ars vivendi

Originalausgabe
Erste Auflage 2005



Text: Prof. Dr. Hartmut Beck
Übersetzungen ins Englische: Valerie Ashe, Adam Lawrence

www.arsvivendi.com



Grafische Gestaltung: Wolfgang Gillitzer, Elisabeth Dötzer, www.gillitzer.net

Umschlaggestaltung: Wolfgang Gillitzer
unter Verwendung eines Fotos von Manfred Gillert: Kaiserburg, Nürnberg

Lithografie: Reprostudio Schmidt, Nürnberg

Druck: Passavia Druckservice, Passau

Printed in Germany

ISBN 3-89716-531-7

*Hartmut Beck*
*Manfred Gillert*

## Nuremberg from the Air

# Nürnberg aus der Luft

ars vivendi

## Einführung

Nicht nur die Besucher, sondern auch die langjährigen Bewohner Nürnbergs, die ihre Stadt gut kennen, sind immer wieder überrascht, welche Überblicke und Einblicke Luftbilder vermitteln können, die aus geringer Flughöhe gemacht wurden. So zeigt sich hinter einer eindrucksvollen Fassade vom Boden aus betrachtet erst aus der Luft die Gestaltung des Baukörpers einschließlich der Dachlandschaft. Auch die größeren Parkanlagen sind nur aus der Vogelperspektive hinsichtlich Ausdehnung und Gestaltungskonzept zu erfassen.

Nürnberg ist mit knapp 500 000 Einwohnern eine weltoffene Stadt mit einer reichhaltigen Geschichte und gilt als »heimliche Hauptstadt Nordbayerns«.

Mit einer Stadtfläche von rund 186 km² beträgt die Ausdehnung in Nord-Süd-Richtung 23,5 km und in Ost-West-Richtung 21,4 km. Die Stadt ist das Zentrum der expandierenden Metropolregion Nürnberg, in der über 2,1 Millionen Menschen leben.

Nürnberg profitiert von der verkehrsgünstigen Lage im Schnittpunkt wichtiger Autobahnen, Bundesstraßen und Bahnlinien in Süddeutschland sowie von der Nähe zu den Ländern Osteuropas.

Jedes Jahr kommen mehr als 20 Millionen Besucher, um die nach den Verwüstungen des Zweiten Weltkrieges in neuer Schönheit erstrahlenden Sehenswürdigkeiten zu bestaunen bzw. an Veranstaltungen in Nürnberg teilzunehmen. Diesen Besucherzahlen und knapp 2 Millionen Übernachtungen pro Jahr ist es zu verdanken, dass der Tourismus einen bedeutenden Wirtschaftszweig mit 850 Millionen Euro Umsatz jährlich und mehr als 13 000 Arbeitsplätzen bildet.

Trotz ihrer Ausdehnung ist Nürnberg eine überschaubare Stadt, in der die 161 ha große Altstadt mit ihrer 5 km langen, gut erhaltenen Stadtmauer den Mittelpunkt bildet. Sie wird beherrscht von der weithin sichtbaren Kaiserburg, die sich als Stadtkrone auf einem Felsen in der Nordwestecke der Altstadt erhebt.

Die von dem Luftbildfotografen Manfred Gillert für diesen Band angefertigten aktuellen Aufnahmen aus 150 bis 300 m Höhe zeigen eine Auswahl der bekanntesten Gebäude, Plätze, Parks und Straßen der Stadt. Die Reihenfolge der Bilder beginnt da, wo die meisten Besucher ihre Tour starten: auf der Burg und in ihrer Umgebung. Dann folgt ein Rundgang durch die von der Pegnitz getrennte nördliche und südliche Altstadtseite, die nach ihren Hauptkirchen St. Sebald und St. Lorenz benannt sind. Über den Plärrer geht es nach Westen zur schnurgeraden Fürther Straße, auf deren Trasse ab 1835 die erste Eisenbahn Deutschlands fuhr. Entlang der südlichen Altstadtmauer führt der Flug zurück in den Osten der Stadt über das Theaterviertel zum Presseviertel und weiter zum Leipziger Platz mit dem markanten Hochhaus. Über den 120 ha großen Marienpark geht es dann nach Norden zum Flughafen und zum landwirtschaftlichen Intensivanbaugebiet des Knoblauchslandes. Von hier aus führt der Flug nach Süden über die Hochhäuser am Wöhrder See hinweg in die Südstadt mit dem Volkspark Dutzendteich, dem Messegelände und dem Hafen. Den Abschluss bilden weithin sichtbare Landmarken wie der Fernsehturm und die Südkaserne sowie Erholungsgebiete wie Luitpoldhain und Tiergarten.

Alle für diesen Band gewählten Motive wurden bei wechselnden Lichtverhältnissen zu verschiedenen Tages- und Jahreszeiten fotografiert.

Nürnberg hat mit den Flusstälern der Pegnitz und Rednitz, dem die Stadt umschließenden Reichswald im Osten und Süden sowie zahlreichen Parks ausgedehnte Grünzonen, was die Luftbilder in eindrucksvoller Weise belegen. Diese von der Bevölkerung zu allen Jahreszeiten gern aufgesuchten Erholungsgebiete tragen wesentlich zur Lebensqualität in der Stadt bei. Auch für die Besucher der Stadt sind sie neben den historischen Monumenten vielbesuchte Attraktionen.

## Preface

WHETHER A FIRST-TIME VISITOR or a long-time resident of Nuremberg, no one can fail to be impressed by low altitude aerial photography of the city. The facade of a building may be impressive at street level, but it is only from the air that the layout of the buildings and rooftops can truly be appreciated. Similarly, the design and extent of the great parks can only be grasped from above. Nuremberg with its 500,000 inhabitants is a cosmopolitan city, rich in history and is seen as the »secret capital of Northern Bavaria«. Covering an area of approximately 186 sq km, the city stretches 23.5 km from north to south and 21.4 km east to west. The city is the centre of the growing metropolitan region of Nuremberg where more than 2.1 million people live.

Nuremberg enjoys good transport infrastructure, with easy access to major motorways, highways and trains in South Germany as well as close proximity to the Eastern European countries.

More than 20 million visitors travel to Nuremberg each year to marvel at the beautiful sights restored to new glory after the devastation of World War II and to participate in local festivals. It is thanks to these visitors and the 2 million nights they spend here per year that tourism is such an important branch of the economy with an annual turnover amounting to 850 million euros and providing employment for more than 13,000 people.

Despite its expansion, Nuremberg is still a pleasant place. The Old City provides a focus, with its 161 hectares surrounded by 5 km of well-preserved city wall. It is overlooked by the »Kaiserburg« (Imperial Castle), clearly visible crowning a hill above the northwestern part of the Old City.

Aerial photographer Manfred Gillert has taken the pictures for this collection at altitudes between 150 and 300 metres. They show a selection of the city's most familiar buildings, squares, parks and streets. Our flight begins where most visitors begin their tour: at the castle and surrounding area. The tour then continues through the northern and southern neighbourhoods of the Old City – separated by the river Pegnitz and named after the great churches of St. Sebaldus and St. Lawrence. Passing over the Plaerrer, our flight takes us west to the remarkably straight Fuerther Strasse, the route of the first German train in 1835. Following the southern part of the city wall, we return to the eastern part of the city. We fly over the theatre district to the press quarter and then on to Leipziger Platz with the prominent tower block. Past the 120 hectares »Marienplatz« the journey then continues on northwards to the airport and to the intensive farming area called »Knoblauchsland« (Garlic Country). From here the flight wings its way southwards, over the tower blocks on Wöhrd Lake to the south of the city and the public park »Volkspark Dutzendteich«, then on to the trade exhibition centre and port. The tour concludes with landmarks that are recognisable even at a distance – the Television Tower, the South Barracks and recreational areas like Luitpoldhain and the »Tiergarten« (zoological gardens).

All the places chosen for this volume were photographed in different light conditions, at various times of the day and at different times of the year.

These aerial photographs make clear the impressive amount of green country that surrounds and permeates Nuremberg – from the numerous parks and the Pegnitz and Rednitz river valleys to the imperial »Reichswald« forest to the south and east of the city. At any time of year, these areas are very popular excursion sites with the locals and significantly add to the quality of life in the city. With visitors, they are just as popular as Nuremberg's historical monuments.

**Burg**
Welch ein stimmungsvolles Winterbild: Von Südwesten aus zeigen sich Burg und Umgebung in seltener Schneepracht! Die ausgedehnte Wehranlage mit 220 m Länge und 50 m Breite liegt auf einem Felssporn in der nordwestlichen Ecke hoch über der Altstadt. Die wohl um 1040 unter dem späteren Kaiser Heinrich III. begonnene Burg gliedert sich von links nach rechts in die Kaiserburg, Reste der Burggrafenburg und reichsstädtische Bauten. Sie ist Nürnbergs bekanntestes Bauwerk.

**Castle**
A wonderfully atmospheric winter scene: a rare view of a snow-covered »Burg« and its surroundings from the southwest! The extensive fortifications measure 220 by 50 metres and are built high over the Old City on a rocky edifice jutting out of its northwest corner. Construction of the castle began around 1040 under the auspices of the later Emperor Henry III. Nuremberg's best known monument is divided into the »Kaiserburg« (Imperial Castle), the remains of the »Burggrafenburg« (Castle of the Governor of the Fortress) and buildings related to Nuremberg's function as an imperial city.

**Burgbasteien**
Die unter Leitung des Maltesers Antonio Fazuni 1538–45 erbauten Burgbasteien sind ein Meisterwerk des Befestigungsbaus. Sie bestehen aus der Hauptbastei links des Kemenatenbaus der Kaiserburg und zwei niederen Basteien vorne. Hinter der geknickt geführten Mauer sind weitere Basteien angelegt. Ein kleeblattförmiger Graben fasst die gesamte Anlage zusammen. Heute sind der Rosengarten auf der Tiergärtnertorbastei vorne und der Burggarten auf der Hauptbastei vielbesuchte Grünanlagen.

**The Castle's Bastions**
The castle's bastions built by Antonio Fazuni of Malta in the years 1538 to 1545 are a masterpiece of fortification architecture. Protecting the Imperial Castle, they consist of a main bastion located to the left of the ladies' wing and two lower bastions in the foreground. More bastions lie behind the zigzag stretch of wall. The construction is bounded by a moat in the shape of a cloverleaf. Today the rose garden on top of the »Tiergärtnertor« bastion (in the foreground) and the castle garden on the main bastion are popular public parks.

**Albrecht-Dürer-Haus**
Im prächtigen Eckgebäude in der Bildmitte schräg gegenüber dem Tiergärtnertorturm lebte der Maler Albrecht Dürer von 1509 bis zu seinem Tod 1528. Das um 1420 erbaute viergeschossige Haus mit hohem Sandsteinsockel und aufgesetztem, spätmittelalterlichem Fachwerk wurde im Zweiten Weltkrieg schwer beschädigt. Nach vorbildlicher Restaurierung und Wiedereröffnung 1949 vermittelt es als Museum einen Eindruck von Leben und Werk des bekanntesten Nürnbergers.

**The House of Albrecht Duerer**
The artist Albrecht Duerer lived from 1509 until his death in 1528 in the splendid house on the corner diagonally opposite the tower of the »Tiergärtnertor«, pictured here in the middle. The four-storey house built around 1420 on high sandstone foundations, with a late-medieval timber framework, was severely damaged in World War II. After its admirable restoration, it was reopened as a museum in 1949, giving an impression of the life and work of Nuremberg's most famous citizen.

**Weißgerbergasse**
Im großen Bogen schwingt eine enge Gasse mit schmucken Fachwerkhäusern durch die westliche Sebalder Altstadt. Mit 22 alten Handwerkerhäusern zählt die Weißgerbergasse zu den am besten erhaltenen Straßen Altnürnbergs. Ehemals stellten hier die Weißgerber nahe der wasserreichen Pegnitz hochwertiges Leder her. Heute ist die malerische Gasse eine Attraktion für Einheimische und Touristen.

**Tawers Lane**
A narrow lane aligned with decorative medieval timber houses curves through the western part of the historic Sebald quarter. With 22 old craftsmen's houses, the Weissgerbergasse is one of the best preserved streets of original Nuremberg. The tawers (white tanners) used to produce high quality leather here near to the river Pegnitz, where water was plentiful. Today the picturesque lane is an attraction for locals and tourists alike.

**Sebalduskirche**
Umgeben von der verschneiten Sebalder Altstadt mit ihrer charakteristischen Dachlandschaft liegt die namengebende Hauptkirche der nördlichen Altstadtseite wie ein Schiff in der Bildmitte. Der gewaltige Bau mit spätromanischem Westchor und zwei imposanten Türmen mit gotischen Spitzhelmen wurde ca. 1230/40 begonnen. Er ersetzte eine Kapelle aus dem 11. Jh. Mit der Nachbarschaft von Rathaus (unten) und Kirche drängen sich hier geistliche und weltliche Macht der Stadt eng zusammen.

**Church of St. Sebaldus**
The great church dominates the centre of this view like a gracious ship. It is surrounded by »Sebald«, the northern part of the Old City named after the church, covered in snow with its characteristic rooftops. Work on the splendid building, with its late Romanic choir to the west and two imposing towers with Gothic spires, began around 1230/40. It replaced a chapel from the 11th century. The proximity of the town hall (below) to the church demonstrates the secular and clerical struggle for power in the town.

**Schürstabhaus**
Das im Zweiten Weltkrieg im Dachbereich schwer beschädigte Schürstabhaus wurde erst 1995–97 restauriert. Das dominierende Eckgebäude auf der Nordseite des Sebalder Platzes geht auf zwei Einzelhäuser aus der Zeit um 1200 bzw. Mitte des 13. Jh. zurück und erlebte mehrere Umbauten. Die heutige Bezeichnung rührt von einer Patrizierfamilie her, die zwischen 1328 und 1478 Hauseigentümer war. Im Haus befinden sich noch gotische Gewölbe, Fresken und Holzsäulen.

**The Schuerstab House**
The roof of the Schuerstab House which was severely damaged in World War II was not restored until 1995–1997. The corner building dominating the northern part of the Sebalder Platz originally consisted of two separate houses dating from around 1200 and 1250 and has been refurbished on several occasions. The current name derives from an aristocratic family who owned the house from 1328 until 1478. Gothic vaults, frescos and wooden beams can still be seen today.

**Fembohaus**
Die 1591–96 errichtete Spätrenaissance-Anlage mit prachtvoller nach Süden gerichteter Fassade ist das einzige Nürnberger Bürgerhaus, das den Zweiten Weltkrieg unzerstört überstand. Das im Auftrag des niederländischen Kaufmanns Philipp van Oyrl errichtete und nach einem späteren Besitzer Fembo benannte Haus an der Burgstraße beherbergt das Stadtmuseum. Im Innern des Hauses befinden sich barocke Stuckdecken und holzvertäfelte Wände.

**Fembo House**
The late-renaissance house with its splendid southfacing facade was built from 1591 to 1596 and was the only town house in Nuremberg to have survived World War II unscathed. Commissioned by the Dutch merchant Philipp van Oyrl but named after its subsequent owner, Fembo, the building on Burgstrasse now houses the municipal museum. Baroque stucco ceilings and wooden panelled walls decorate the interior.

**Hauptmarkt**
Der Hauptmarkt, der schönste und bedeutendste Platz Nürnbergs, beherbergt in der Adventszeit mit dem Christkindlesmarkt den bekanntesten deutschen Weihnachtsmarkt. Vor der prächtigen Kulisse der gotischen Frauenkirche erstreckt sich die beleuchtete Budenstadt aus Tuch und Holz. Die einzigartige Atmosphäre lockt alljährlich rund 2,5 Millionen Besucher an. Im Vordergrund steht der 19 m hohe Schöne Brunnen mit gotischem Figurenschmuck.

**Old Town Marketplace**
The Hauptmarkt is the most beautiful and important square in Nuremberg and home to Germany's most famous Christmas Market (»Christkindlesmarkt«) during Advent. This brightly lit market of wooden stalls offering handicrafts and snacks is set against an impressive backdrop of the Gothic »Frauenkirche« (Church of Our Lady). The unique atmosphere attracts around 2.5 million visitors every year. In the middle at the front is the 19 metres high »Schöner Brunnen« or Beautiful Fountain with its Gothic figurines.

**Altes Rathaus**
Von Nordwesten her ist der ausgedehnte Komplex des Alten Rathauses zwischen der Theresienstraße unten und dem Rathausplatz in der Mitte oben zu sehen. 1616–20 errichtete der Baumeister Jakob Wolff der Jüngere den mächtigen Bau. Er brachte mit der Formensprache der italienischen Spätrenaissance einen bis dahin unbekannten Hauch von Italien in die Stadt. Das hohe Dach gegenüber gehört zur Sebalduskirche, deren Fassade gerade renoviert wird.

**Old Town Hall**
Looking from the north west we can see the sprawling complex of the Old Town Hall between Theresienstrasse below and the Rathausplatz (Town Hall Square) in the upper centre. The architect Jakob Wolff junior built this impressive building between 1616 and 1620. By using a particular style from the Italian late-renaissance period, he introduced a touch of Italy which the city had not previously known. Opposite is the high roof of the Church of St. Sebaldus which is just having its facade redone.

**Insel Schütt**
Zwischen den modernen Dächern einer Schule unten und dem mittelalterlichen Schuldturm der vorletzten Stadtbefestigung oben sind kleine Holzbuden und Zelte zu sehen. An zwölf Tagen im Herbst findet auf der Insel Schütt das Nürnberger Altstadtfest statt. Zum »schönsten Treffpunkt des Jahres« kommen weit über eine Million Besucher zum Schauen und Feiern. Die Pegnitzinsel lohnt aber zu allen Jahreszeiten einen Besuch.

**Schuett Island**
The medieval »Schuldturm« (Debtor's Prison) at the top of the view was once part of the penultimate city fortifications. In this view, wooden stalls and tents fill the space between the ancient prison and the modern school rooftops below. Every autumn, Schuett Island plays host to the twelve days of Nuremberg's »Altstadtfest« (Old City Festival), and more than a million visitors come to party and absorb unique atmosphere at the »event of the year«. Whatever the season, the island in the river Pegnitz is well worth a visit.

**Heilig-Geist-Spital**
Der Blick von der Museumsbrücke unten auf das Heilig-Geist-Spital ist eines der meistfotografierten Motive in Nürnberg. 1339 stiftete Konrad Groß für 200 sieche und arme Leute ein Spital zwischen den Pegnitzarmen. Durch Erweiterungen bis 1525 erhielt das Heilig-Geist-Spital sein heutiges Aussehen. In der Kapelle wurden 1423–1796 die Reichskleinodien verwahrt. Noch immer befindet sich im Spital u. a. ein Altenheim, das den Stiftungsgedanken aufrechterhält.

**Holy Ghost Hospital**
The view from the Museum Bridge looking onto the Holy Ghost Hospital is one of the most popular spots for a photograph in Nuremberg. In 1339, Konrad Groß endowed a hospital for 200 poor and sick people between the two arms of the river Pegnitz. The present building is the result of extension work undertaken in 1525. The Imperial Regalia were kept in the chapel from 1423 until 1796. In keeping with the spirit of the original endowment, the hospital is now among other things a home for the elderly.

**Wöhrder Wiese**
Das sommerlich heitere Bild zeigt einen Ausschnitt der Wöhrder Wiese mit dem nördlichen Pegnitzarm. Sie liegt zwischen dem Wöhrder Talübergang und dem Pegnitzeinfluss in die Altstadt und ist ein beliebtes, ganzjährig aufgesuchtes Naherholungsgebiet. Seit einigen Jahren veranstaltet hier das Amt für Kultur und Freizeit im Sommer das »Erfahrungsfeld der Sinne« mit wechselnden Themen. Ein mobiler Biergarten mit bunten Schirmen am Eingang dient der Geselligkeit und Erholung.

**Woehrd Meadow**
This bright summertime picture shows a section of the Woehrd Meadow along the northern arm of the river Pegnitz. A popular recreational area all year round, the meadow lies between the Woehrd viaduct and the spot where the Pegnitz flows into the Old City. Every summer the Department of Culture and Leisure organises the »Experience of the Senses« exhibition on the Woehrd Meadow, taking a different theme each year. A mobile beer garden with brightly coloured parasols provides the ideal spot to relax in good company.

**Trödelmarkt**

Wie ein Schiff liegt die Trödelmarktinsel zwischen zwei Pegnitzarmen. Nur die Karlsbrücke und zwei Stege verbinden sie mit den beiden Altstadthälften. Seit dem 16. Jh. fand hier der Verkauf von Alt- und Gebrauchtwaren oder »Trödel« statt; 1809/10 erhielt sie daher die Bezeichnung Trödelmarkt. Die heutige Bebauung der Insel mit kleinen Häusern stellt den gelungenen Versuch dar, nach der völligen Zerstörung 1945 wieder an die frühere Idylle anzuknüpfen.

**Flea Market**

Flea Market Island is docked like a ship between two arms of the river Pegnitz. Only the Charles Bridge and two footbridges connect the island to both sides of the Old City. From the 16th century onwards, antiques and second hand goods or »Trödel« (jumble) were sold here, hence in 1809/10 the island received the name »Trödelmarkt«. The current complex of small houses on the island is a successful attempt at recreating the former idyll that was completely destroyed in World War II.

**Egidienplatz**
Zwei mächtige Gebäude begrenzen den Ausschnitt des leicht ansteigenden Egidienplatzes. Rechts die barocke Saalkirche St. Egidien (1718) mit zwei Türmen. Sie entstand auf den Mauern der 1696 abgebrannten ehemaligen Klosterkirche der Benediktiner. Links dahinter, ein monoton wirkender Nachkriegsbau. An seiner Stelle stand das weltberühmte Pellerhaus (1605). Es galt mit seinem reichen Fassadenschmuck und Ziergiebel als eines der repräsentativsten Bürgerhäuser Deutschlands.

**St. Giles Square**
Two prestigious buildings border the clip showing the slightly inclining Egidienplatz. On the right is the Baroque hall Church of St. Giles (1718) with its two towers. It was built on the remains of the former Benedictine abbey, which burnt down in 1696. To the left, behind it, is a dull postwar building built on the site of the world famous Peller House (1605). With its richly decorative facade and ornamental gable, it was deemed to be the best typical example of Germany's town houses.

**Tucherschloss**
Von Bäumen umgeben liegt das Tucherschloss in einer kleinen Gartenanlage. 1533–44 ließ sich die Patrizierfamilie Tucher vom Architekten Peter Flötner einen Sommersitz am Treibberg errichten. Das sowohl von der Spätgotik als auch von der italienischen Renaissance geprägte Gebäude wurde am 2. Januar 1945 zerstört. Die Familie Tucher baute 1965–68 das kleine Schloss in reduzierter Form wieder auf. Es beherbergt heute die Verwaltung der Städtischen Museen.

**Tucher Mansion**
Surrounded by trees, Tucher Mansion is situated in a small park. From 1533 until 1544 the aristocratic Tucher family employed the architect Peter Flötner to build a summer residence at Treibberg. The building, showing influences not just of the late Gothic but also the Italian Renaissance period, was destroyed on 2nd January 1945. The Tucher family rebuilt a smaller version of the mansion from 1965 to 1968. It now houses the administration department of the municipal museums.

**WiSo-Fakultät**
Welch ein Kontrast in der Nordostecke der Sebalder Altstadt! Zwischen der Stadtmauer mit dem runden Laufer Schlagturm und Wohnhauszeilen mit roten Steildächern liegen die modernen Bauten der Wirtschafts- und Sozialwissenschaftlichen Fakultät der Universität. Das 1976 bezogene Gebäude mit seiner ungewöhnlichen Dachlandschaft erhielt 2001–03 einen 94 m langen Erweiterungsbau im Vordergrund. Hier studieren rund 5 000 junge Menschen aus vielen Ländern.

**Faculty for Economics and Social Science**
The northeastern corner of Sebald in the Old City is a place of contrasts. Sandwiched between the city walls, the round tower Laufer Schlagturm and the rows of houses with their steep red rooftops we find the university's Faculty of Economics and Social Science. The modern building with its unusual roof profile was first occupied in 1976, and was given a 94 metres long extension in 2001–2003 (in the foreground). Around 5,000 young people from all over the world study here.

**LGA-Gebäude**
Auf dem Gewerbemuseumsplatz in der Bildmitte erhebt sich das massige Karree des Sandsteinbaus der ehemaligen Landesgewerbeanstalt (LGA). Es wurde nach Plänen von Theodor von Kramer 1892–97 errichtet. Der viergeschossige Bau im Stil der italienischen Spätrenaissance wurde nach Kriegsbeschädigungen ohne seine beherrschende Kuppel wieder erstellt. Nach Auszug der LGA und Umbau 1996–97 ist der Bau heute Sitz des Bildungszentrums der Stadt sowie des Presseclubs.

**LGA Building**
This view of the Gewerbemuseumsplatz (Tradecrafts Museum Square) shows the solidly built sandstone building which used to house the Landesgewerbeanstalt (LGA, a public organisation for business services and quality assurance). The four-storey building in late Italian renaissance style was built according to plans laid out by Theodor von Kramer between 1892 and 1897. After being damaged in the war, it was rebuilt without its prominent dome. The LGA subsequently moved out and since its refurbishment in 1996–1997 the building now houses the city's education centre and the press club.

**Grand Hotel**
Die markante Fassade des Grand Hotels beherrscht die nordöstliche Seite des Bahnhofsplatzes. Das 1896 eröffnete Fünf-Sterne-Haus mit 186 Gästezimmern, fünf Sälen, Konferenzzimmern sowie einem bekannten Restaurant wurde durch Bomben schwer beschädigt. Nach Beschlagnahme durch die Amerikaner wurde es 1954 wiedereröffnet. 1980 verkaufte die Familie Lotz das Hotel an eine internationale Hotelkette, 1996 wechselte es zu Le Méridien und wurde mit 15 Millionen Euro renoviert.

**Grand Hotel**
The distinctive facade of the Grand Hotel dominates the north-eastern side of the Bahnhofsplatz (station square). The five star hotel with 186 rooms, five ballrooms, conference facilities and a well known restaurant opened in 1896. After serious bomb damage and being impounded by the Americans, it reopened in 1954. In 1980 the Lotz family sold the hotel to an international chain of hotels, in 1996 it changed hands to Le Méridien and was refurbished at a cost of 15 million euros.

**Hauptbahnhof**
Mit über 110 000 Fahrgästen pro Tag ist der Hauptbahnhof der am stärksten frequentierte Bahnhof in der Stadt. Durch seine Lage am Bahnhofsplatz gegenüber dem Frauentor ist er ein idealer Ausgangspunkt für einen Besuch der Altstadt. Der 1900–05 erstellte neobarocke Muschelkalkbau mit hoher Vierkantkuppel wurde im Zweiten Weltkrieg stark zerstört. Bei der Anlage des U-Bahnknotens unter dem Gebäude wurde 1970–71 die Kuppel in niedrigerer Form wiedererrichtet.

**Main Station**
The busiest station in the city is visited by more than 110,000 passengers each day. Its location at the Bahnhofsplatz opposite the Frauentor (Lady's Gate) provides an ideal starting point for a visit to the Old City. The neo-Baroque shell limestone building with its high square cupola was built during 1900–05 and severely damaged in World War II. A smaller version of the cupola was rebuilt when a major station for underground trains was built under the site in 1970–71.

**Königstor**

Wie ein Wächter flankiert der 40 m hohe »Dicke Turm« des Königstors den Eingang in die Altstadt. Gegenüber an der Königstraße erstreckt sich der lange Bau des Künstlerhauses im historisierenden Stil (1906–08) mit dem modernen Kopfbau (2000/01). Das helle geschwungene Gebäude im Hintergrund ist das Neue Museum (1996–99) am Klarissenplatz. Im Handwerkerhof links vom Turm laden Kunsthandwerker mit ihren Werkstätten seit 1971 zum Schauen und Kaufen ein.

**King's Gate**

The 40 metres high »Dicke Turm« (Thick Tower) watches over the King's Gate entrance to the Old City. Facing it across the Koenigstrasse is the long Artists' House in historicist style (1902–08) with a modern lobby (2000/01). The bright curved building in the background is the New Museum (1996–99) on Klarissenplatz. In the Tradesmen's Courtyard to the left of the tower, craftspeople have been inviting the public to look at their workshops and purchase their wares since 1971.

**Mauthalle**
Welch ein Gegensatz zwischen den modernen Warenhäusern Kaufhof (1950) rechts sowie Hertie (1956) oben, heute City Point, und der mittelalterlichen Mauthalle am Hallplatz! Der auf dem vorletzten Stadtgraben erbaute ehemalige reichsstädtische Kornspeicher mit fünfgeschossigem Dachboden (1498–1502) wurde 1897–98 zu einem Geschäftshaus mit Läden im Erdgeschoss umgebaut. 1945 brannte die Mauthalle völlig aus und wurde 1951–53 in vereinfachter Form wieder aufgebaut.

**Toll House**
The modern department stores Kaufhof (1950, right) and Hertie (now City Point, 1956, above) contrast starkly with the medieval Toll House on Hallplatz. The former imperial granary with its five-storey attic was originally built 1498–1502 on the site of the penultimate city moat. It was redeveloped in 1897–98 for commercial use with shops on the ground floor. In 1945 the Toll House was devastated by fire and a simpler version was rebuilt in 1951–53.

**Nassauer Haus**
Das markante Nassauer Haus gegenüber der Lorenzkirche ist das einzige erhaltene mittelalterliche Turmhaus in Nürnberg. Der Keller und die beiden ersten Geschosse stammen vermutlich aus dem späten 12. Jh. Die zwei oberen Geschosse mit den Eck-Erkern und dem Wappenfries datieren aus dem 15. Jh. Die Rundbogenöffnungen im Erdgeschoss wurden ab 1836 angebracht. Nach erheblichen Kriegsschäden wurde das Nassauer Haus in nur wenigen Jahren wiederhergestellt.

**Nassau House**
The distinctive Nassau House opposite the Church of St. Lawrence is the only intact medieval tower house in Nuremberg. The cellar and the first two floors probably date back to the late 12th century. The upper two floors with the corner bay windows and the frieze with the coat of arms are of 15th century origin. The arched entrances on the ground floor were built after 1836. It took just a few years to rebuild the Nassau House after it had suffered serious damage in the war.

**Dachlandschaft der Lorenzer Altstadt**
In der klein strukturierten, geschlossen wirkenden Dachlandschaft der Lorenzer Altstadt mit roten Satteldächern fallen einige größere Bauten mit störenden Dächern auf: Es handelt sich um Warenhäuser. Der trapezförmige Bau rechts oben ist der Kaufhof (1950) an der Königstraße, daneben das ehemalige Hertie-Kaufhaus (1956), heute City Point (1999). Nur teilweise sichtbar liegt unten an der Karolinenstraße das Modehaus Breuninger (2003).

**Roof Top View of the St. Lawrence part of the Old City**
Among the seemingly small roof tops of St. Lawrence, set close together and with red gabled roofs, there are some noticeably larger buildings with very different roof tops: these are the department stores. The trapezoid at the upper right is Kaufhof (1950) in the Koenigstrasse, next to it the former Hertie department store (1956), now City Point (1999). Partly visible is the fashion house Breuninger (2003) below in the Karolinenstrasse.

**Lorenzkirche**
Aus der Karolinenstraße fällt der Blick auf die in der 2. Hälfte des 14. Jh. entstandene prächtige Westfassade von St. Lorenz mit Statuenportal, Fensterrose und Ziergiebel. Die gewaltigen Dimensionen des hochgeführten Langhauses dahinter lassen sich im Vergleich mit der umgebenden Bebauung erkennen. Am 81 m hohen Südturm finden gerade Renovierungsarbeiten statt. Die Lorenzkirche wird auch wegen ihrer einzigartigen Kunstschätze viel besucht.

**Church of St. Lawrence**
In the Karolinenstrasse our eyes are drawn to the impressive west facade of the late 14th century Church of St. Lawrence and its statuesque main portal, rose window and decorative gables. A comparison with the surrounding buildings gives an indication of the huge dimensions of the tall nave behind. The 81 metres high south tower is in the process of being renovated. St. Lawrence Church is a popular attraction because of its unique art treasures.

**Kornmarkt**
Mit einem auffälligen Bodenmuster aus Basaltlava und veredeltem Betonstein präsentiert sich zwischen hohen Gebäuden der westliche Teil des Kornmarktes. Das Bild zeigt einen Ausschnitt des großzügigen Vorplatzes des Germanischen Nationalmuseums, der 2001/02 neu gestaltet wurde. Das Tor links unten ist der Eingang zur »Straße der Menschenrechte« von Dani Karavan, die 1993 mit 23 weißen Stelen in der Kartäusergasse geschaffen wurde.

**Corn Market**
The western section of the Corn Market with its striking floor pattern of basalt and concrete blocks is flanked by two tall buildings. The picture shows part of the generous forecourt of the National Museum of German Art and Culture, which was redesigned in 2001/2002. The gate at the lower left leads to the 23 white columns of the »Street of Human Rights« created in the Kartaeusergasse by Dani Karavan in 1993.

**Germanisches Nationalmuseum**
Das Germanische Nationalmuseum ist die größte zusammenhängende bauliche Anlage innerhalb der Altstadt. Das größte deutsche Museum für Kunst und Kulturgeschichte entstand 1857 in einem 1525 aufgelösten Kartäuserkloster und einer Kirche (oberhalb der Bildmitte). Mit den Jahren kamen immer mehr Gebäude hinzu. Die jüngste Erweiterung ist der aus der Luft wie ein »E« aussehende Bau von 1993 an der Kartäusergasse.

**National Museum of German Art and Culture**
The National Museum is the largest complex of buildings in the Old City. The biggest German museum of art and cultural history was built in 1857 in what was originally a Carthusian monastery (dissolved in 1525) and in a church (top of the picture in the middle). Over the years even more buildings have been added. The most recent extension is a building built in 1993 in the Kartaeusergasse which looks like the letter »E« from the air.

**Katharinenkloster**
Das von Dominikanerinnen 1294 gegründete Katharinenkloster wurde im Zweiten Weltkrieg völlig zerstört. Während die Klosterkirche als mahnende Ruine bis heute erhalten blieb, entstanden auf den Grundmauern des Klosters davor und dahinter Neubauten. In ihnen ist die Stadtbibliothek untergebracht. Im Sommer lockt die Kirchenruine mit ihrem besonderen Charme viele Besucher zu Konzerten und Theateraufführungen an.

**St. Catherine's Monastery**
St. Catherine's Monastery was created in 1294 by Dominican nuns and was completely destroyed in World War II. Whilst the ruins of the monastery's church have been left as they are as a lasting memorial, in front of and behind it new buildings have been built on the original foundations of the monastery's other buildings. The city library is located in one of them. In summer the church ruins with their particular charm are a popular place for concerts and theatre productions.

**Weinstadel – Henkersteg**
Über die Maxbrücke hinweg fällt der Blick auf das mächtige Gebäude des Weinstadels, auf den Wasserturm und den Henkersteg. Der 1446–48 errichtete Bau des Weinstadels diente als Sondersiechenhaus für Leprakranke, seit 1571 als Weinlager. Heute beherbergen das Haus und der Turm, ein Relikt der vorletzten Stadtbefestigung aus der 2. Hälfte des 13. Jh., ein Studentenwohnheim. Der hölzerne Henkersteg wurde 1457 über den südlichen Pegnitzausfluss gebaut.

**Wine Storehouse – Hangman's Bridge**
Across the Max Bridge, our attention is drawn to the impressive building of the Wine Storehouse, to the Water Tower and Hangman's Bridge. Built in 1446–48, the Wine Storehouse served as a special hospital for lepers until 1571, when it became a wine depot. Today the building and the tower, which is a relic of the penultimate city fortifications from the late 13th century, provide student housing. The wooden Hangman's Bridge was built in 1457 across the southern arm of the river Pegnitz.

**Unschlittplatz**
Der Unschlittplatz wurde 1828 durch das hier aufgetauchte Findelkind Kaspar Hauser weit über Nürnberg hinaus bekannt. Der Platz wird im Osten dominiert vom 55 m langen Unschlitthaus mit viergeschossigem Satteldach und typischen Schleppgauben. Es wurde 1490–91 von Hans Beheim dem Älteren auf dem alten Stadtgraben als reichsstädtischer Kornspeicher gebaut. Die historischen Fachwerkhäuser gegenüber wurden 1978–81 mit Hilfe der Altstadtfreunde saniert.

**Unschlittplatz**
Unschlittplatz achieved notoriety far beyond Nuremberg when the famous foundling Kaspar Hauser mysteriously appeared here in 1828. The eastern side of the square is dominated by the 55 metres long Unschlitt House with a four-storey gabled roof and dormer windows. It was originally built as an imperial granary on the old city moat in 1490–91 by Hans Beheim senior. The historical timbered houses opposite were restored in 1978–81 by the Friends of the Old City of Nuremberg.

**Weißer Turm mit Brunnen**
Kraftvoll erhebt sich der Weiße Turm aus der Fußgängerzone nahe dem Jakobsplatz links oben. Er ist ein Relikt der vorletzten Stadtbefestigung aus dem 13. Jh. Der Name rührt von der Farbe her, mit der man früher das Backsteinmauerwerk kaschiert hat. Davor erkennt man den Hans-Sachs-Brunnen mit den realistischen Figuren des Ehekarussells. Er wurde 1984 von Prof. Jürgen Weber nach einem Gedicht des Handwerkerpoeten von 1541 geschaffen.

**White Tower with Fountain**
The sturdy White Tower stands in the pedestrian zone near to the Jakobsplatz, upper left. It is part of the remains of the previous city fortifications dating from the 13th century. The name stems from the white paint which used to cover the red brick walls. In front, in clear view, is the Hans Sachs Fountain with the realistic figures depicting the ups and downs of married life. It was created in 1984 by Prof. Jürgen Weber based on a Hans-Sachs-poem from 1541.

**Jakobsplatz**
Zwei Kirchen beherrschen den Jakobsplatz: im Vordergrund die mittelalterliche, von der Gotik geprägte evangelische Jakobskirche und ihr gegenüber die im klassizistischen Stil gehaltene katholische Elisabethkirche. Sie wurde erst 1803 fertig gestellt. Am Jakobsplatz stand ehemals ein königlicher Wirtschaftshof. Er bildete neben demjenigen am Egidienberg die zweite südlich der Pegnitz gelegene Keimzelle Nürnbergs.

**St. James Square**
Two churches dominate the Jakobsplatz: St. James and St. Elizabeth. St. James is medieval, gothic and protestant; while the catholic Church of St. Elizabeth was built in the classicist style and completed in 1803. Jakobsplatz was originally a royal farmyard. It was the second main hub of activity in Nuremberg south of the river Pegnitz after St. Giles Square (Egidienplatz).

Männer aufgepasst!

Hamburg-Mannheimer
Coca-Cola

**Plärrer**
Der Plärrer an der Südwestecke der Altstadt ist eine der Verkehrsdrehscheiben der Stadt. Von hier aus fuhr 1835 die erste deutsche Eisenbahn ins 6 km entfernte Fürth. Heute kreuzen mehr als 80 000 Autos den Platz und viele Fahrgäste steigen in U-Bahnen, Straßenbahnen und Busse ein bzw. aus. Die Platzanlage wird beherrscht vom 56 m hohen Plärrer-Hochhaus (1954) im Westen, das lange Zeit das höchste Bürogebäude Bayerns war.

**Plaerrer**
The Plaerrer, a square to the southwest of the Old City, is one of the main traffic junctions in Nuremberg. In 1835, the first German train left here heading for Fuerth, 6 km away. Now, more than 80,000 cars cross Plaerrer daily, and many more passengers step in and out of the underground trains, trams and busses. The west side of the square is dominated by the 56 metres high Plaerrer tower (1954) which was the tallest office block in Bavaria for many years.

**Fürther Straße**
Das Bild zeigt ein Teilstück der boulevardartigen Fürther Straße kurz nach Beginn am Plärrer. Die schnurgerade Straße wurde 1801–04 als Chaussee zur Nachbarstadt Fürth durch die damalige preußische Besatzungsmacht angelegt. Ab 7. Dezember 1835 fuhr parallel zu ihr die Ludwigsbahn als erste deutsche Eisenbahn, die 1922 von der Straßenbahn abgelöst wurde. In den 80er Jahren wurde diese von der U-Bahn verdrängt, die im westlichen Teil oberirdisch verläuft.

**Fuerther Strasse**
The picture shows part of the boulevard-like Fuerther Strasse near its source at the Plaerrer. The remarkably straight road was built by the occupying Prussian forces in 1801–04 as an avenue leading to the neighbouring city of Fuerth. The Ludwig railway – the first in Germany – ran parallel to this road from 7th December 1835 until its replacement by trams in 1922. In the 1980s, the trams in turn gave way to the underground trains, which travel above the surface in the western part of the city.

**Justizpalast**
Wie ein kleiner Stadtteil an sich wirkt aus der Luft das »Justiz-Karree« mit dem monumentalen Justizpalast an der Fürther Straße. Der 1908 begonnene, 350 m lange Bau wurde 1916 von König Ludwig III. eröffnet. Hier fanden 1945–46 die Nürnberger Prozesse statt, in denen die Hauptverantwortlichen des NS-Regimes verurteilt wurden. Heute sind in mehr als 600 Räumen rund 1500 Menschen an verschiedenen Gerichten beschäftigt.

**Palace of Justice**
From the air, the »Law Courts« with the monumental Palace of Justice on the Fuerther Strasse look like a small separate neighbourhood. Started in 1908, the 350 metres long building was opened in 1916 by King Ludwig III. In 1945–46 the Nuremberg trials were held here where those mainly responsible for the Nazi regime were sentenced. Now more than 600 offices and courtrooms house around 1,500 people working in various courts.

**Johannisfriedhof**

Der 1234 erstmals erwähnte Johannisfriedhof gilt als der schönste und bedeutendste Friedhof in der Stadt. Seit 1520 werden alle Gräber mit Sandsteinen bedeckt und im Sommerhalbjahr mit überwiegend roten Blumen geschmückt. Viele tragen noch die historischen Bronze-Epitaphe mit Inschriften und Wappen. Berühmte Bewohner Nürnbergs wie Albrecht Dürer ruhen hier. Das Bild zeigt einen Ausschnitt des Friedhofs mit der Johanniskirche (1377–95).

**St. John's Cemetery**

St. John's Cemetery, first mentioned in 1234, is widely considered the most beautiful and important cemetery in the city. Since 1520 all the graves have been covered with sandstone monuments and during the summer months these are decorated with red flowers. Many still have historical bronze epitaph plaques with engravings and coats of arms. Famous citizens of Nuremberg such as Albrecht Duerer rest here. The picture shows a part of the cemetery with St. John's Church (1377–95).

**Hesperidengärten**
Die Hesperidengärten im Stadtteil St. Johannis sind ein Juwel barocker Gartenkultur. Die bis zu 200 m langen Gärten erstrecken sich hangabwärts zur Pegnitz. Mit üppigem Skulpturenschmuck und Brunnen nach italienischem Vorbild versuchten die reichen Patrizier die Atmosphäre fürstlicher Gärten zu schaffen. Die von der Johannisstraße rechts oben zugänglichen Anlagen sind gern besuchte Oasen der Ruhe, aber auch stimmungsvolles Ambiente für Konzerte.

**Hesperian Gardens**
The Hesperian Gardens in the neighbourhood of St. John's (»St. Johannis«) are a beautiful example of Baroque gardening culture. The gardens slope almost 200 metres down towards the river Pegnitz. The wealthy patrician aristocracy tried to recreate the atmosphere of princely gardens in Italian style using opulent sculptures and fountains. The gardens which can be accessed from the Johannisstrasse, top right, are a very popular retreat for peace and quiet, but they also provide an idyllic ambience for concerts.

**Theaterviertel**
Vom Frauentorgraben, einem Teilstück des vielbefahrenen Altstadtrings, erstreckt sich das Theaterviertel am Richard-Wagner-Platz gen Süden. Rechts das neobarocke Opernhaus mit der mächtigen Kuppel (1903–05), links der moderne Bau des Schauspielhauses mit den Kammerspielen (1957–59). Im lang gestreckten Bau dazwischen sind Werkstätten und Verwaltung untergebracht. Im Herbst 2003 wurden die bis dahin Städtischen Bühnen Nürnbergs zum Staatstheater erhoben.

**Theatre District**
The theatre district at the Richard-Wagner-Platz stretches southwards from the Frauentorgraben (Moat of the Lady's Gate) which is part of the very busy ring road round the historical centre. To the right is the neobaroque Opera House with the impressive cupola (1903–1905), to the left the modern theatre (1957–1959). The long stretched-out building inbetween houses the workshops and administration. In the autumn of 2003 the then City Theatres of Nuremberg were elevated in status to become a state theatre.

Café im Staatstheater

**Verkehrsmuseum**

Das ehemalige Verkehrsmuseum ist heute Sitz des DB-Museums und des Museums für Post und Kommunikation. Die umfangreichen Sammlungen im Hauptgebäude in der Bildmitte enthalten einige der ältesten und wertvollsten technikgeschichtlichen Exponate Europas. Ein ausgedehntes Freigelände mit Bahnanschluss liegt links außerhalb des Bildes. Der Eingangsbereich zu den Museen in der Lessingstraße gegenüber der Rückseite des Schauspielhauses ist unten zu sehen.

**Transport Museum**

The former Transport Museum is now home to the German Railway Museum and the Museum of Communication. The main building shown in the picture houses the lion's share of the extensive collections, including some of Europe's oldest and most valuable technological exhibits. To the left, outside the picture, is an extensive open-air exhibition ground with it's own connection to the rail network. The entrance to the museum is in Lessingstrasse, opposite the rear side of the theatre. It can just be seen at the lower edge of the picture.

**Arbeitsamt**
Das 1991 eröffnete Arbeitsamt, eines der damals größten im Bundesgebiet, neben dem Theaterviertel im Hintergrund. Die quadratischen Baukörper haben mit 80 m Seitenlänge und vier bis sechs Geschossen beachtliche Dimensionen. Ab 2002 begann mit dem Abriss älterer Häuser entlang der Tafelfeldstraße eine Erweiterung in Richtung zum rechten Bildrand.

**Job Centre**
The job centre, shown here with the theatre in the background, was opened in 1991 as one of the largest job centres in the region. The square structure with four to six storeys measures an impressive 80 metres along each side. The demolition of older buildings along the Tafelfeldstrasse began in 2002, making way for an extension towards the right hand side of the picture.

AXA

**Presseviertel**
Im Laufe von über 50 Jahren entstand zwischen der breiten Marienstraße vorne, der Gleißbühlstraße oben und dem rechten Bildrand das Presseviertel. Keimzelle der *Nürnberger Nachrichten* (NN) war das angeschnittene Gebäude mit Portikus unten, derzeit Sitz der Geschäftsleitung des Verlags Nürnberger Presse. Im Pressehaus gegenüber befinden sich die Redaktionen von NN, *Nürnberger Zeitung* und *Sonntagsblitz*, im hellen Bau rechts davon entlang der Badstraße diejenige von *kicker Sportmagazin*.

**Press District**
Over the course of more than 50 years, the press district has developed until it stretches from the broad Marienstrasse (foreground) and the Gleissbuehlstrasse (above) to the right hand border of the picture. The »Nuernberger Nachrichten« (*Nuremberg News* or *NN*) started out in the porticoed building partly visible at the lower right of the picture. Today, this structure houses the management of the »Nürnberger Presse« publishing house. The Press House opposite contains the editorial offices of the *NN*, the *Nuernberger Zeitung* and »Sonntagsblitz«. The light-coloured building to its right, along the Badstrasse, is home to the »Kicker Sportmagazin«.

**Adcom Center**
Entlang der Badstraße erstreckt sich zwischen der Bahnhofstraße vorn und dem Willy-Brandt-Platz hinten der mächtige Block des Adcom Centers. Der vom Architekten Prof. Reindl entworfene moderne Bürokomplex mit Großparkhaus unter der Parkanlage entstand ab 2001 im Auftrag der Münchener Industriebau (DIBAG) auf dem zentralen Busbahnhof der Stadt. Ein kleiner Busbahnhof im Innenhof des Adcom Centers knüpft an diese Tradition an.

**Adcom Centre**
The impressive Adcom Centre on the Badstrasse sprawls between the Bahnhofstrasse in the foreground and Willy-Brandt-Platz behind. Professor Reindl was commissioned by the Münchener Industriebau (Munich Industrial Construction Company, DIBAG) to design the modern office building and car park, and it was built in 2001 on the site of the former central bus station. A small bus station in the courtyard of the Adcom Center maintains the traditional purpose of the site.

**»Parcside«-Komplex**
Wie ein schwungvoll geschriebenes »H« sieht der »Parcside«-Komplex aus der Luft aus. Das moderne, bis zu siebengeschossige Büro- und Geschäftshaus wurde von den Grazer Architekten Szyszkowitz und Kowalski entworfen und im Juni 2004 von den ersten Nutzern bezogen. Das an der südlichen Ecke des Stadtparks stehende Gebäude mit 8 000 m² Gewerbefläche weist viele Bezüge zur Grünanlage auf; so kann man z. B. mit etwas Fantasie im »Parcside« die Form eines Baumes erkennen.

**»Parcside« Complex**
From the air, the »Parcside« Complex looks like a curved letter »H«. The modern, seven-storey office and shopping complex was designed by the Graz architects Szyszkowitz and Kowalski, and first occupied in June 2004. The building is situated in the southern corner of the city park and offers 8,000 square metres of office space. The design shows many references to the park – with a little imagination, one can recognise the shape of a tree in the »Parcside« Complex.

**Sternwarte**
Die nach Plänen von Otto Seegy 1930–31 erbaute städtische Sternwarte auf dem Rechenberg im Osten der Stadt ist eine der schönsten und größten Volkssternwarten in Deutschland. Sie hat nach einer kriegsbedingten Unterbrechung erst 1952 ihren Betrieb wieder aufgenommen. Das Bild zeigt das eindrucksvolle Gebäude bei geöffneter Kuppel. Im Hintergrund sind Teile einer Kleingartenanlage zu sehen, die in der Nachkriegszeit entstand.

**Observatory**
Built in 1930–31 to designs by Otto Seegy, the public observatory on Rechenberg hill in the eastern part of the city is one of the largest and most beautiful in Germany. After closing during the war, it was not put into operation again until 1952. The picture shows the impressive building with the dome open. In the background there are small garden allotments which were set up after the war.

**Stadtpark mit Restaurant**
Das Bild zeigt einen Ausschnitt des 19 ha großen Stadtparks mit Weiher und Restaurant. Nach der totalen Verwüstung der Grünanlage im Zweiten Weltkrieg legte das Stadtgartenamt unter Kurt Ahles den Park nach einem Plan von 1958 neu an. Dabei entstand auch der attraktive Neubau des Restaurants mit Sälen und Terrassengarten. Es ist nicht nur für die Nordstadt ein beliebter Treffpunkt.

**City Park with Restaurant**
The picture shows a clip of the 19 hectares city park with its lake and restaurant. After the park was totally destroyed in World War II, the city's Parks Department, under the guidance of Kurt Ahles, rebuilt the park according to plans dating from 1958. At the same time, the restaurant was built as an attractive new building, with function suites and terraced patios. It is a popular meeting place for people from all over the city.

BUS

**Leipziger Platz**
Zwei Gebäude beherrschen optisch den Leipziger Platz: das 13-geschossige Merian Forum (2001–02) und das geschwungene, auf Stelzen stehende Delphinhaus (1994–98) auf der Südseite hinter der U-Bahn-Station. Das etwas gedrungen wirkende, knapp 42 m hohe Bürohochhaus hat eine Nutzfläche von rund 5 300 m². Die neugestaltete Platzanlage mit zentralem Brunnen wurde im Mai 2003 eingeweiht und ist schon nach kurzer Zeit ein beliebter Treffpunkt geworden.

**Leipziger Platz**
Two buildings visually dominate the Leipziger Platz: the 13 storey Merian Forum (2001–2002) and the curved Dolphin House (1994–1998) which stands on stilts on the southern side of the square behind the underground station. The somewhat squat office block, almost 42 metres high, has around 5,300 square metres of office space. The newly refurbished square with its central fountain was opened in May 2003 and has quickly become a popular local meeting place.

**Nordostbahnhofsiedlung**
Wie ein Fächer sind die Wohnblöcke der großen Nordostbahnhofsiedlung entlang der Hauptachse der Leipziger Straße angeordnet. Die Siedlung wurde nach Plänen von Karl Sorg 1929–31 als Teil des kommunalen Wohnbauprogramms errichtet. Seit einigen Jahren werden die Blöcke modernisiert, den erreichten Stand verraten die roten Dächer. Die hellen Gebäude rechts gehören zum Theresienkrankenhaus, das ab 1928 an der Mommsenstraße entstand.

**Northeast Station Housing Estate**
The housing blocks of the extensive Northeast Station Housing Estate spread out like a fan along the main thoroughfare of the Leipziger Strasse. The estate was designed by Karl Sorg 1929–31 as part of the municipal home building programme. For some years, modernisation work has been taking place – the red roofs show how far the refurbishment has progressed. The light-coloured buildings to the right are part of St. Theresa's Hospital, which was built in the Mommsenstrasse in 1928.

**Nordostpark**
Eine Ansammlung ungewöhnlicher Bauten an einer Kreuzung! Es handelt sich um einen Teil des 27 ha großen Nordostparks begrenzt von der Äußeren Bayreuther rechts und der Thurn-und-Taxis-Straße links. In der »Denkfabrik des 21. Jahrhunderts« mit u. a. dem Weltkompetenzzentrum für Optoelektronik des US-Konzerns Lucent Technologies sollen einmal 10 000 Menschen forschen und entwickeln. Das s-förmige Wellenhaus unten markiert unübersehbar den Eingang zur Stadt.

**North-Eastern Park**
A collection of unusual buildings. It is part of the 27 hectares North-Eastern Park which borders onto the outer Bayreuther Strasse on the right hand side and the Thurn-und-Taxis-Strasse on the left. The »Thinktank of the 21st Century« houses, among other things, the World Competency Centre for Optoelectronics for US giant Lucent Technologies. One day, 10,000 people will research and develop here. The S-shaped building below is an unmistakable gate to the city.

**Marienbergpark**
Von 1933 bis 1943 war der Marienberg Standort des ersten Nürnberger Flughafens. Nach seiner Verlegung nach Norden entstand 1953–73 auf dem 120 ha großen Gelände südlich der Marienbergstraße links ein Freizeitpark im Stil eines englischen Landschaftsparks für die Bewohner der Nordstadt. Die stimmungsvolle Herbstaufnahme zeigt im Vordergrund den künstlich angelegten Weiher und den Marienbuck, der als Aussichts- und Rodelberg genutzt wird.

**Marienberg Park**
From 1933 until 1943 Marienberg was the site of Nuremberg's first airport. After this activity was transferred further north, the residents of northern Nuremberg were able to benefit from a new park in the style of English country-house grounds. It was set up from 1953 to 1973 on a 120 hectares site just south of the Marienbergstrasse. This atmospheric autumnal picture shows the man-made pond in the foreground and Marienbuck hill, where people can go tobogganing or just enjoy the view from the summit

**Flughafen**
Das von Südosten aufgenommene Bild zeigt einen Ausschnitt des Flughafens, der 1955 eröffnet wurde. Heute schon ein ausgedehnter, urbaner Komplex mit U-Bahn-Anschluss, wird er noch immer weiter ausgebaut. Hinter den Parkfeldern steht eine Reihe von Parkhäusern, dahinter liegt der zentrale Empfangsbereich mit den Abfertigungshallen. Mit rund 3,3 Millionen Passagieren jährlich hat der internationale Flughafen Nürnberg einen großen Einzugsbereich bis nach Thüringen und Sachsen.

**Airport**
The picture taken from south-east shows part of the airport which was opened in 1955. Still growing today, it is now a sprawling urban complex with a connection to the underground railway. Behind the open-air car park we see a further row of multi-storey car parks, and behind them the main terminal with the arrivals and departure lounges. With around 3.3 million passengers every year, Nuremberg International Airport has a wide catchment area reaching as far as Thuringia and Saxony in eastern Germany.

**Tabakanbau im Knoblauchsland**
Seit 1654 wird im Knoblauchsland, einem landwirtschaftlichen Intensivanbaugebiet im Norden der Stadt, nachweislich Tabak angebaut. Die Flächen dieser Sonderkultur stehen seit 1970 unter Vertrag und unterliegen der EG-Marktordnung. Im Bild sind die charakteristischen lang gestreckten Folien-Trockenzelte umgeben von Tabakfeldern zu sehen. In ihnen werden die zwischen Mitte Juli und Mitte September stufenweise reifenden Blätter der Tabakstauden luftgetrocknet.

**Tobacco Growing in »Knoblauchsland«**
There is evidence to show that tobacco has been cultivated since 1654 in »Knoblauchsland« (Garlic Country), an intensive farming area north of the city. The special fields have been licensed and subject to European Community regulations since 1970. The picture shows the typical long plastic drying tents surrounded by tobacco fields. The leaves of the tobacco bushes are air-dried here after gradually ripening from mid July to September.

**Schloss Neunhof**
Am Rand von Neunhof im Knoblauchsland liegt das nach dem Dorf benannte kleine Schloss mit einem Barockgarten. Das Ende des 15. Jh. erbaute ehemalige Wasserschloss ist einer der am besten erhaltenen der zahlreichen Herrensitze in Nürnberg. Es besitzt noch originale Ausstattung aus dieser Zeit in den Innenräumen. Heute gehört das Schloss zum Germanischen Nationalmuseum und ist im Sommerhalbjahr zu besichtigen. Deutlich ist im Bild der ehemalige Wassergraben zu erkennen.

**Neunhof Mansion**
On the outskirts of Neunhof in Knoblauchsland is a small mansion with a baroque garden. Built towards the end of the 15th century and previously surrounded by water, Neunhof Mansion is one of the best preserved of the many manor houses in Nuremberg. Inside, it still has the original fittings and furnishings of the period. Today the mansion belongs to the National Museum of German Art and Culture and is open to the public during the summer months. The picture clearly shows the path of the former moat.

**Wöhrder See**

Der durch den Aufstau der Pegnitz entstandene Wöhrder See besteht aus zwei Teilen: dem Unteren See (1972–75) und dem Oberen See (1975–81). Er hat eine Gesamtfläche von 52 ha bei einer mittleren Tiefe von 1,9 m. Die Aufnahme zeigt die leere Wasserfläche im Herbst vom Seeausfluss am Wöhrder Wehr unten bis zum Seebeginn im Hintergrund. Gut erkennbar sind die Uferwege und einige der Freizeiteinrichtungen in der umrahmenden Grünzone sowie die 25 m hohe Fontäne im See.

**Woehrd Lake**

Woehrd lake is the result of a dam built across the river Pegnitz. It consists of two parts: the lower lake (1972–1975) and the upper lake (1975–1981) which together cover 52 hectares with an average depth of 1.9 metres. The photograph shows the lake in autumn, stretching from the Woehrd outflow weir at the lower right up to the source of the lake in the background. We can clearly see the footpaths around the lake and the leisure facilities in the surrounding park, as well as the 25 metres high fountain.

**Wohnanlage Noricus**
Auf dem hügeligen Gelände der Zeltner-Brauerei, die im Luftkrieg zerstört wurde, entstand in den 60er Jahren an der Ostendstraße die Wohnanlage Noricus. In den Wohnhochhäusern mit maximal 65 m Höhe leben in rund 700 Eigentumswohnungen ca. 2000 Menschen. Die Nähe zum Stadtzentrum und die günstige Lage auf der Südseite des Wöhrder Sees machen die Wohnanlage attraktiv. Auch der einmalige Blick über die Altstadt hinweg zur Burg trägt zur Beliebtheit bei.

**Noricus Housing Estate**
The Noricus Housing Estate in the Ostendstrasse was built in the 1960s, on the hilly site of the bombed-out Zeltner brewery. Around 2,000 people live in approximately 700 privately owned flats in blocks up to 65 metres high.The proximity to the city centre and the convenient position on the southern banks of Woehrd Lake make the estate an attractive location. The estate is especially popular for its unique view of the Old City reaching up to the castle.

**Wöhrder Seeausfluss**
Umrahmt von buntem Herbstlaub präsentiert sich der Ausfluss der Pegnitz aus dem Wöhrder See am gleichnamigen Talübergang. Links oben sind die jüngsten Bauten der Fachhochschule zu sehen, unten das HDI-Hochhaus (1989–91), zwei ineinander gestellte Bürotürme mit 55 bzw. 45 m Höhe, und ein Hotelanbau. Das Gebäude gegenüber ist der ehemalige Verwaltungsbau des Milchhofs, der von Otto Ernst Schweizer 1930 erbaut wurde.

**Woehrd Outflow**
At the point where Woehrd Lake flows into the river Pegnitz, the Woehrd Bridge is surrounded by colourful autumnal foliage. In the upper left we see the new buildings of the »Fachhochschule« (University of Applied Sciences). In the lower foreground is the HDI insurance tower (1989–1991) made of two joined office blocks 55 and 45 metres high, with an extension housing a hotel. The building opposite used to house the offices of the dairy company, and was built by Otto Ernst Schweizer in 1930.

**Zeltnerschloss**
Herbststimmung rund um das Zeltnerschloss im Stadtteil Gleißhammer. Das auf einen Herrensitz des Spätmittelalters zurückgehende Wasserschloss brannte im Zweiten Weltkrieg völlig aus und wurde 1955 wieder aufgebaut. Es zählt zu den reizvollsten Herrensitzen Nürnbergs. Die im Besitz der Stadt befindliche Anlage wird als Kultur- und Bildungszentrum genutzt.

**Zeltner Mansion**
Autumnal moods at the Zeltner Mansion in Gleißhammer. This manor house, surrounded by a moat, goes back to the late Middle Ages. It was burnt to the ground in World War II and then rebuilt in 1955. One of the most beautiful manor houses in Nuremberg, the city-owned building is now used as a cultural and educational centre.

**Business Tower**
Bis zum Herbst 2003 war der 135 m hohe Business Tower das höchste Bürogebäude Bayerns. Der von 1998 bis Mitte 2000 erstellte 34-geschossige, schlanke Turm ist ein eindrucksvoller Bau. Er steht in der Nordwestecke des Bürokomplexes der Nürnberger Versicherung auf einem 3,2 ha großen Areal am Mittleren Ring im Hintergrund. Für die Nürnberger Wirtschaft symbolisiert der Büroturm die Aufbruchstimmung im wiedervereinigten Deutschland in den 90er Jahren.

**Business Tower**
The 135 metres high Business Tower was the tallest office block in Bavaria until the autumn of 2003. Built between 1998 and mid 2000, it is an impressive, lean building with 34 floors. Situated on the Middle Ring road in the north-western corner of the »Nuernberger Versicherung« (Nuremberg Insurance) office complex, it stands on an area measuring 3.2 hectares. For Nuremberg business, the office block symbolises the 1990's feeling of optimism in a reunited Germany.

**Bundesagentur für Arbeit**
Die auffälligen, bis zu 78 m hohen Baukörper der ehemaligen Bundesanstalt für Arbeit, heute Bundesagentur für Arbeit (BA), sind weithin im Stadtbild Nürnbergs sichtbar. Mit ihrer Gestaltung und den spiegelnden Glasfassaden repräsentieren die 1973 bzw. 1992 eröffneten Bauten auch optisch eine neue Generation von Bürohochhäusern. Die lange Zeit höchsten Bürogebäude der Stadt beherbergen den Sitz der BA und das Landesarbeitsamt Bayern.

**Federal Employment Agency**
The striking 78 metres tall buildings of the former German Labour Exchange (»Bundesanstalt für Arbeit«), now called the Federal Employment Agency (»Bundesagentur für Arbeit«, »BA«), are clearly visible on Nuremberg's cityscape. The architectural style with reflecting glass facades represented a new generation of office buildings when they were opened in 1973 and 1992. The office block which for a long time used to be the tallest in the city, is home to the headquarters of the »BA« and the Bavarian Employment Agency.

**Volkspark Dutzendteich**

Weit schweift der Blick von der Münchener Straße unten nach Nordosten über den Volkspark Dutzendteich zur Kongresshalle. Der 1947 entstandene See rechts ist die einstige Baugrube für das hier einmal geplante Deutsche Stadion des NS-Regimes. Von links ziehen sich Flachweiher, Kleiner und Großer Dutzendteich bis zum oberen Rand. Die zahlreichen Camper in der größten Grünanlage Nürnbergs sind Besucher der Großveranstaltung »Rock im Park«.

**Dutzendteich Public Park**

The view reaches a long way from the Muenchener Strasse below to the north east, across the public park Dutzendteich up to the Congress Hall. The lake on the right was created in 1947 by flooding the building site of the Nazi regime's planned German Stadium. From the left, there is the shallow pond, then the Smaller and Greater Dutzendteich ponds reaching to the top border. The numerous campers in Nuremberg's biggest park are visiting the major »Rock in the Park« festival.

**Dokumentationszentrum**
Die Aufnahme zeigt ein Detail aus dem folgenden Bild, allerdings aus einem anderen Blickwinkel. Im November 2001 eröffnete Bundespräsident Johannes Rau das Dokumentationszentrum, in dem die Ausstellung »Faszination und Gewalt« gezeigt wird. Das nach Plänen von Prof. Günther Domenig aus Graz im umgestalteten Nordflügel der Kongresshalle eingerichtete »Doku-Zentrum« veranschaulicht die Funktion der Reichsparteitage in Nürnberg innerhalb des NS-Staates.

**Documentation Centre**
The photograph shows a close-up of the picture to follow, but from a different angle. In November 2001, the President of the Federal Republic of Germany, Johannes Rau, opened the Documentation Centre showing the exhibition »Fascination and Terror«. The Documentation Centre set up in the northern wing of the Congress Hall after refurbishing according to the plans by Professor Günther Domenig from Graz, illustrates the function of the Nazi party rallies held in Nuremberg within the Nazi state.

**Kongresshalle**
Das hufeisenförmige Monument der Kongresshalle ist mit 275 m Länge und 265 m Breite ein gewaltiges Bauwerk. Der von Ludwig Ruff nach dem Vorbild des römischen Kolosseums geplante Bau sollte 50 000 Zuschauer fassen. Als markanter Teil des Reichsparteitagsgeländes dient der Torso heute kulturellen Zwecken. Während Großveranstaltungen wie dem Norisringrennen werden der Innenhof und das Volksfestgelände dahinter als Parkplätze genutzt.

**Congress Hall**
The horseshoe-shaped Congress Hall is a huge construction measuring 274 metres long and 265 metres wide. The building was designed by Ludwig Ruff along the lines of the Roman Colosseum and was supposed to hold 50,000 spectators. Originally one of the main features of the Nazi party rally ground, the main body is now used for cultural events. The courtyard and the fairground are used as car parks during major events like the Noris Ring races.

**Zeppelinfeld**
Über das Dach der Arena hinweg fällt der Blick nach Norden auf die Relikte der NS-Bauten auf dem Zeppelinfeld, so benannt seit der Landung eines Luftschiffs 1909. Auf der fast quadratischen Anlage (289 m x 312 m) entstanden nach Plänen des Architekten Albert Speer nach dem Vorbild des Pergamonaltars die lang gestreckte Haupttribüne und davor die u-förmigen 6,5 m hohen Zuschauerwälle mit 34 Türmen. Heute wird die Tribüne zu Veranstaltungen, die Wiese als Sportfläche genutzt.

**Zeppelin Field**
Beyond the roof of the Arena, our attention is drawn northwards to the relics of Nazi architecture on the Zeppelin Field, named after the airship which landed here in 1909. Albert Speer's design of the long main platform was inspired by the Pergamon Altar. In front we can see the U-shaped spectator tribunes, 6.5 metres high with 34 towers, surrounding the roughly square site (289 metres x 312 metres).

**Städtisches Stadion**
Die ersten Sportbauten auf dem Zeppelinfeld entstanden 1921–28 als öffentliche Notstandsmaßnahmen. In der Bildmitte die bekannteste Sportanlage, das Städtische Stadion, auch Frankenstadion genannt. Hier spielt der ruhmreiche 1. FC Nürnberg, der »Club«. Für die Fußballweltmeisterschaft 2006, bei der Nürnberg beteiligt ist, werden wieder einmal Umbauten im Stadion vorgenommen. Links am Rand die neue Arena, eine Multifunktionsanlage.

**City Stadium**
The first sport sites were built on the Zeppelin Field from 1921–28 as emergency public measures. In the middle of the picture is modern Nuremberg's best known sports facility, the city stadium or Franconia Stadium. This is the home of the famous Nuremberg football team known as the »Club«. The stadium will be refurbished anew for Nuremberg's participation in the 2006 FIFA World Cup. At the extreme left is the new Arena, a multi-functional complex.

ARO
mister•lady•jeans
Adecco
Coca-Cola
ODDSET

**Messegelände**
Eingerahmt von der Großen Straße rechts, der Karl-Schönleben-Straße unten, der Münchener Straße links und dem bewaldeten Silberbuck liegt das Messegelände. Mit derzeit 150 000 m² Ausstellungsfläche in Hallen wurde es seit der Eröffnung 1974 immer wieder erweitert. Nürnberg zählt mit seinem Messezentrum neben Hannover, Frankfurt, Köln, Düsseldorf, München und Berlin zur kleinen Gruppe der deutschen Großmessen. Weltweit rangiert die Messegesellschaft mit ihrem Umsatz derzeit auf Platz 18.

**Exhibition Centre**
The Exhibition Centre is framed by the Grosse Strasse to the right, the Karl-Schoenleben-Strasse below, the Muenchener Strasse to the left and the woods of the Silberbuck hill above. Since its opening in 1974, the centre has been continually extended until it now offers 150,000 square metres of exhibiting space. Nuremberg's exhibition centre is one of an elite group of major German exhibition centres that includes Hannover, Frankfurt, Cologne, Duesseldorf, Munich and Berlin. The company running the exhibition centre currently ranks 18th in the world in turnover terms.

## Kongress Center Ost

Eine Reihe wuchtiger Baukörper entlang der Großen Straße! Es handelt sich um die jüngsten Bauten im Osten des Messegeländes. Vorn das vom Architekten H. Seipel entworfene sternförmige, sechsgeschossige Kongress Center Ost, das 60 Mio. Euro gekostet hat. Es bietet Platz für bis zu 3 200 Menschen und erhöht die Kongresskapazitäten der Nürnberger Messe auf 11 000 Gäste. Dahinter die hohe transparente Halle 7, das Servicecenter und die zwei Parkhäuser mit braunen Dächern.

## Conference Centre East

A row of massive buildings along the Grosse Strasse. These are the new buildings to the east of the Exhibition Centre. In the foreground is the star-shaped, six-storey Conference Centre designed by the architect H. Seipel and built at a cost of 60 million euros. There is enough space for 3,200 people, increasing the conference capacity of the Nuremberg Exhibition Centre to 11,000 guests. Behind are the tall, transparent Hall No. 7, the Service Centre and the two multi-storey car parks with brown roofs.

**Langwasser-Zentrum**
Die Aufnahme zeigt einen Ausschnitt des Zentrums von Langwasser mit dem Heinrich-Böll-Platz an der Glogauer Straße und der evangelischen Paul-Gerhardt-Kirche gegenüber. Von links drängt die 1969 eröffnete zentrale Einkaufseinrichtung, heute Franken-Center, ins Bild, unten rechts das Gemeinschaftshaus. Das 6 km von der Altstadt entfernte Langwasser mit knapp 40000 Einwohnern entstand ab 1954 als Trabantenstadt im Grünen.

**Langwasser Centre**
The picture shows part of the Langwasser Centre with the Heinrich-Böll-Platz on the Glogauer Strasse and the protestant Paul Gerhardt Church opposite. On the left, pushing its way into the picture is the central shopping centre, opened in 1969, now called the »Franken-Center«. At the lower right is the community centre. Langwasser has almost 40,000 inhabitants and lies 6 km from the Old City. It was created as a green-belt satellite town in 1954.

**Parkwohnanlage Neuselsbrunn**
Nach Plänen des Architekten Gerhard Dittrich errichtete eine Düsseldorfer Wohnbaugesellschaft ab 1963 im Norden Langwassers die Parkwohnanlage Neuselsbrunn mit rund 700 Wohnungen. Die 14 ha große durchgrünte Anlage liegt in einem Straßendreieck und hat U-Bahn-Anschluss im Bild links unten. Die Wohnanlage wird optisch dominiert von einer Gruppe von Hochhäusern, deren höchstes 22 Geschosse hat. Heute leben in Neuselsbrunn ca. 1400 Menschen.

**Neuselsbrunn Park Estate**
Following designs by the architect Gerhard Dittrich, a Duesseldorf construction company started building the 700 flats of the Neuselsbrunn Park Estate north of Langwasser in 1963. The 14 hectares estate is landscaped with parks. Located on an important road junction, it has its own underground station as can be seen to the lower left. The estate is visually dominated by a group of tower blocks, the highest with 22 floors. Around 1,400 people now live in Neuselsbrunn.

**Südklinikum**
Der gewaltige Komplex des Klinikums Nürnberg Süd (1994) liegt wie ein Raumschiff auf einer Lichtung im Wald. Mit 1022 Betten und rund 2350 Beschäftigten ist das Krankenhaus eine kleine Stadt an sich auf einem Areal von 16,5 ha. Hier werden über 40000 Patienten pro Jahr bis zur höchsten Versorgungsstufe betreut. Die SO-Aufnahme zeigt vorne den Patientengarten und hinten die Eingangszone zur Breslauer Straße.

**Southern Clinic**
The massive complex of Nuremberg's Southern Clinic (1994) sits like a grounded space ship in a clearing in the forest. The hospital has 1,022 beds and employs around 2,350 people. It is like a small town, covering an area of 16.5 hectares. Each year comprehensive care is provided for 40,000 patients. The picture shows the patients' garden in the foreground and entrance area facing the Breslauer Strasse at the rear.

**Hafen mit Passagierschiffen**
In einem Bogen schwingt sich der Main-Donau-Kanal zum Hafen Nürnberg-Roth, der jenseits der parallel verlaufenden Hafenstraße rechts oben beginnt. Der Ausschnitt zeigt 6 Passagierschiffe, die in der Nähe der Abfertigungsstelle festgemacht haben. Im 1972 eröffneten Hafen, mit 2 $km^2$ Fläche das größte Logistikzentrum Süddeutschlands, legen seit einigen Jahren im Zuge des boomenden Flusstourismus zwischen Rhein und Donau häufiger luxuriöse Kabinenschiffe an.

**Port with Passenger Boats**
The Main-Danube Canal curves round towards the port of Nuremberg-Roth which begins above right on the other side of the harbour road running parallel to the canal. The picture shows 6 passenger boats moored ready to take on guests. The booming tourist industry between the rivers Rhein and Danube has seen luxurious cabin boats docking more often over the past few years in the port, which was opened in 1972. Covering a site measuring 2 sq km the port is the largest logistics centre in south Germany.

**»Mississippi Queen«**
Seit Mai 1996 liegt die »Mississippi Queen« nahe der Schleuse Nürnberg auf dem Main-Donau-Kanal vor Anker. Bis 1994 fuhr der prächtige alte Schaufelrad-Dampfer noch auf dem Mississippi, dem größten Fluss Nordamerikas. Das 58 m lange und 11 m breite Schiff beherbergt auf drei Decks mehrere Restaurants und einen Dancing Club. Im Ersteren wird die kulinarische Vielfalt des amerikanischen Südens im dazu passenden Ambiente geboten, im Letzteren lockt eine Dixieland-Kapelle.

**»Mississippi Queen«**
The »Mississippi Queen« has been docked near to the Nuremberg lock on the Main-Danube Canal since 1996. Only two years earlier, she was still travelling on the Mississippi, the largest river in North America. The splendid old paddle steamer measures 58 metres by 11 metres, and houses several restaurants and a dancing club on her three decks. The restaurants provide typical American southern cuisine in an appropriate atmosphere, while the dancing club boasts a Dixieland band.

**Fernmeldeturm**
Der Fernmeldeturm ist mit 292 m Höhe das höchste Bauwerk Nürnbergs. Er war nach seiner Fertigstellung 1980 mit damals 285 m der dritthöchste Turm im Bundesgebiet. In der 49 m hohen Kanzel, die in Anlehnung an die eiförmige Form der ersten Taschenuhr, dem »Nürnberger Ei«, konzipiert wurde, befinden sich fernmeldetechnische Anlagen. Die nach Norden gerichtete Aufnahme zeigt rechts die Gustav-Adolf-Straße, im Hintergrund das Versandhaus Quelle mit Turm an der Fürther Straße.

**Television Tower**
The 292 metres Television Tower is the tallest building in Nuremberg. When it was completed in 1980, its (then) 285 metres made it the third highest tower in Germany. Telecommunication systems are situated in the 49 metres high platform level, which was designed to be reminiscent of the first pocket watch, the »Nuremberg Egg«. The north-looking view shows Gustav-Adolf-Strasse on the right. In the distance we can see the Fuerther Strasse tower belonging to Quelle, the mail order company.

**Südkaserne**
Das H-förmige Hauptgebäude der ehemaligen Südkaserne erhebt sich wie eine mächtige Landmarke an der Frankenstraße. Die 1935–37 erbaute Kaserne auf einem 17,5 ha großen Areal war eine der modernsten ihrer Zeit. Sie diente zur Sicherung der Reichsparteitage auf dem nahen Märzfeld. Nach aufwendigen Umbauarbeiten (1994–2000) bezog das Bundesamt für Migration und Flüchtlinge den unter Denkmalschutz stehenden Bau, den zuvor die US-Army als Kaserne genutzt hatte.

**South Barracks**
The H-shaped building of the former South Barracks forms a prominent landmark on Frankenstrasse. When the 17.5 hectares barracks were built during 1935–37 they were one of the most modern buildings of their time. They provided security for the Nazi party rallies on the Maerzfeld nearby. After the war the building was used by the US army as barracks until major restoration work from 1994 to 2000. The listed building now houses the Federal Office for Migration and Refugees.

**Tiergarten**
Der Tiergarten am Schmausenbuck gilt als der schönste Landschaftszoo Europas. Im hügeligen Gelände mit Teichen leben auf über 60 ha Fläche mehr als 2500 Wildtiere, darunter auch die einzigen Delphine Süddeutschlands. Die Herbstaufnahme zeigt einen Ausschnitt mit dem Aquazoo. In den vier Becken sind Robben, Pinguine, Biber und Fischotter untergebracht. Mit jährlich über 1 Million Gästen hat der Zoo die höchste Besucherzahl aller Einrichtungen in der Stadt.

**Zoological Gardens**
The zoological gardens on the Schmausenbuck hill are considered to be the loveliest landscaped zoo in Europe. Sixty hectares of hills and ponds provide a home for more than 2,500 wild animals, including the only dolphins in southern Germany. The photograph taken in autumn shows the section with the Aquazoo. Sea lions, penguins, beavers and otters are housed in the four pools. With 1 million visitors, the zoo is the city's single most popular attraction.

**Freiluftkonzert im Luitpoldhain**
Seit einigen Jahren finden Ende Juli und Anfang August im Erholungsgebiet Luitpoldhain »Klassik Open Air«-Konzerte des Staatstheaters Nürnberg statt. Mehrere zehntausend Menschen lagern dann im Gras, verzehren die mitgebrachten Speisen und Getränke und genießen die Musik in den meist lauen Sommernächten. Der Ausschnitt mit der Bühne vermittelt einen Eindruck von diesen beliebten Veranstaltungen im parkartigen Luitpoldhain.

**Open-air Concert in Luitpoldhain**
For several years, the State Theatre of Nuremberg has held »Open Air Classic« Festivals at the end of July and beginning of early August. During the usually mild summer evenings, thousands of people lie on the grass, eat picnics and enjoy the music. This view of the stage gives an impression of these popular events in the parklike Luitpoldhain recreational area.

**Die Autoren**

MANFRED GILLERT, geboren 1953 in Rüdersdorf bei Berlin, lebt schon seit 1961 in Nürnberg und ist längst zum Franken geworden. Nach seiner Lehre als Fotograf bei Bischof & Broel in Nürnberg und seiner Meisterprüfung 1981 leitet er seit 1984 als Geschäftsführer die Firma mit den Schwerpunkten Luftbild, Architektur, Werbung, Messe- und Ausstellungswesen. Für zahlreiche Bildbände über Nürnberg, Mittelfranken und das Fränkische Seenland fertigte er die aktuellen Luftaufnahmen an.

HARTMUT BECK, geboren 1940 in Neustadt/Aisch, lebt seit 1963 in Nürnberg. Nach dem Studium der Wirtschafts- und Sozialwissenschaften sowie der Geografie war er zunächst in der Marktforschung beschäftigt. Nach Tätigkeiten an den Universitäten in Erlangen-Nürnberg und Duisburg arbeitet er seit 1981 wieder als Hochschullehrer an der Universität in Nürnberg. Er ist Autor und Herausgeber zahlreicher Buchpublikationen, darunter auch Bildbände mit historischen und aktuellen Luftaufnahmen von Nürnberg, Fürth und Franken.

**The Authors**

MANFRED GILLERT, born in 1953 in Rüdersdorf near Berlin, has been living in Nuremberg since 1961 and has long since become a local Franconian. He trained as a photographer at Bischof & Broel in Nuremberg and became a master craftsman in 1981. Since 1984 he has been director of the company specialising in aerial photography, architecture, advertising and exhibitions. He has taken photographs of Nuremberg, Central Franconia and the Franconian Lakelands for numerous illustrated books.

HARTMUT BECK, born in 1940 in Neustadt/Aisch, has been living in Nuremberg since 1963. After studying economics, social science and geography, he started work in market research. After working at the universities of Erlangen-Nuremberg and Duisburg he became a university lecturer at the University of Nuremberg in 1981. He is an author and editor of several publications, among them illustrated books with historic and modern aerial photographs of Nuremberg, Fuerth and Franconia.